MW01428237

An Endless Tapestry

Julia Nunnally Duncan

For Rhonda
with best wishes –
Julia Nunnally Duncan

March Street Press
3413 Wilshire
Greensboro NC 27408
marchstreetpress.com
rbixby@earthlink.net
isbn 1-59661-075-1

I would like to thank Joan Aleshire and Fred Chappell for their advice on certain poems.

These poems, sometimes in different form and with different title, were originally published in the following:

Long-Haired Boy, Her Sister's Shoes, Player Piano, Garden Creek, Slingshot, and Fate in *Victoria Press*
Heat and Fever in *Birmingham Poetry Review*
Sharp-Shinned Hawk in *Blue Pitcher*
The Kiss in *Potato Eyes*
Curse in *Warren Wilson Review*
My Father Watches the Red Skelton Show, Porch Swing, Silo, and Seed Catalog[1] in *The Lyricist*
Gathering Dirt in *Gryphon*
My Cousin in *Under Courthouse Hill*
Far Pasture in *A Carolina Literary Companion*
Mountain Boy and Earth in *International Poetry Review*
Wedding Day and Lists[1] in *Appalachian Heritage*
Visit from Her Son[1] in *Only Morning in Her Shoes*
Brown Lung in *Z Miscellaneous*
Patchwork in *Georgia Journal*
Sparrow Hawk in *Katuah*
Apples[2] in *Cold Mountain Review*
Tennessee Baptism, 1915 in *Old Hickory Review*
Tent Revival in *Wayah Review*
Prayer for Rain in *The Arts Journal*

[1]Lists, Visit from Her Son, and Seed Catalog reprinted in *North Carolina Writers & Books* (ncarts.org)
[2]Apples reprinted in *Cold Mountain Review*, 35th Anniversary Issue

I

Long-Haired Boy 3
Heat 5
Sharp-Shinned Hawk 6
Fever 8
The Kiss 9
Curse 10
My Father Watches
The Red Skelton Show 11
Gathering Dirt 13
Her Sister's Shoes 15
Player Piano 17
Garden Creek 19
My Cousin 21
Eight O'Clock 23
Porch Swing 24
Slingshot 26
Silo 28
My Daughter
Ponders Death 31
Ritual 34

II

Fate 39
Far Pasture 42
Mountain Boy 43
Wedding Day 44
Lists 45
Visit from Her Son 46
Seed Catalog 47
Brown Lung 48
March Flowers 49
Patchwork 51
Sparrow Hawk 52
Earth 53
Apples 54
Tennessee Baptism, 1915 55
Tent Revival 57
Prayer for Rain 58

An Endless Tapestry is dedicated to
the memory of my father, Otto Nunnally

I

A Night of Memories

Rose Aylmer, whom these wakeful eyes
May weep, but never see,
A night of memories and sighs
I consecrate to thee.

Rose Aylmer, Walter Savage Landor

Long-Haired Boy

Today I think of you
my savior,
my blond friend and lover,
whose image was created
in my lonely girlhood mind.

Through the years my heart
has been tossed and tumbled.
I have wanted to die
and longed to live;
I have regressed into past lives
I'd hoped to have experienced,
but arrived back here
in my small-town Southern life.
I've hardly thought of you
until now,
and today
the sharp breeze of mid-September
that stirs my wind chimes
and waits for wood smoke
to lift into October skies
reminds me of you.
Of you, I think
and wonder
and look at pastures I pass
and recall how I waited for you
to rise from the crest of a hill
to walk down to me.
I still look.
I still wait.

Once I watched for you
on the festive streets of Asheville,
thought I passed you at Christmastime.
Is it you? I asked
when a young man passed
in turtleneck and bellbottoms,
whose hair hung on his shoulders,
who hummed *Kicks*.
Where are you,
oh long-haired boys of my girlhood?
Where are you,
my own long-haired boy?
Is your hair now gray;
is your brow now furrowed?

I don't care—
I still look.
I still wait.

Heat

He stood at the grave,
a May wind lifting
his dark blond hair.
His eyes may have shown
indifference or despair—
I couldn't tell
for his sunglasses,
though I stared at him
from the crest of the hill
where I stood at a Confederate's grave.
The grave at his feet
was an old one too,
its obelisk hinting
of wealth and devotion.
Devotion must be what brought us here,
I might have said to him
as he caught my gaze and held it
for a moment,
then looked away at the farmland
that stretched beyond sloping plots,
as mute as stone.
Could you be my lover? I wanted to ask,
some yearning rising inside me,
or at least sit in my car
and talk a while?
He could lay his suit jacket
in the empty back seat,
roll his shirt sleeves up
in the heat.

Sharp-Shinned Hawk

The sharp-shinned hawk picked at
the limp body of the sparrow,
and my husband said to go away,
the sight would upset me.
But I watched as it tore at the feathery throat,
picked the dull eyes;
my husband was proud of his careful training,
the weeks of swinging the lure,
whistling into the echoing blue sky
to call the hawk back home.

I was afraid of the hawk—
its anxious bobbing head,
the cat-green eyes that warned me
Don't stare at me; don't stand too close—
and it swooped at my moccasins,
tan leather like its lure;
suddenly I was its prey
as it struck my head,
blond hair in its talons.

I stood in the field of dying grass,
peering toward the evening sky;
my husband beside me swung the lure;
"Sharpie," he called. "It's gone," he said,
his face grim.
Then a spot appeared near a rose-tipped cloud;
"Eep, eep," it cried and circled high,
flogged by blue jays as it tried to descend.
And I whistled to it,
imitating my husband's pitch;
I whistled and watched as we called it home.

Fever

The song I hummed
to send you to rest,
though the way your head
sank deep into the pillow
told me you were far away already,
is a tune I have forgotten.
But I recall that night of moonlight,
its glow making you look like a child
as I brushed your hair from your brow
to press a wet washcloth there.
Suddenly you opened your eyes
and reached your arm to me:
Love me, you said,
and by the way you looked beyond me
I knew the fever was talking.
But I didn't question you
though even your words
I love you—I love you
echoed beyond me.
It didn't matter—
to hear them was enough.

The Kiss

The new-mown grass in the park
stuck to our clothes,
and the dew held the smell of spring.
I knew by the way you reached
and grasped my shoulder
and looked at me, long and melancholy,
that you were going to kiss me.
And when your mouth pressed against mine,
softer than I could have recalled,
I dangled over an abyss for a moment
and then dropped in the darkness,
silent and deep,
falling through time
until we reached the bottom together
and you pulled away,
the moisture of your mouth
on mine.

Later as we ate our sandwiches
I started to ask you
if the kiss gave you pleasure,
if the desire made you feel alive again;
but you looked distracted,
your eyes turned to the reflection of trees
in the pond,
and I left well enough alone.

Curse

I go to the woods near our house
and sit on a fallen log, mossy and damp,
till you find me there.
Why do you sit here alone? you ask,
and I see in your eyes,
dark and steady as the shadows around us,
that you do not understand.
When I say *I don't know—I guess*
I'm lonely,
I might as well have struck you.
And we sit together for a while,
the creek talking to itself
or to the hemlock that towers over us.
When you say *Let's go in now;*
the air's getting colder
and the breeze has picked up,
I ask to stay a while longer.
Alone? you ask.
It's o.k., I say
before you turn to leave.
But as you follow the path to the house,
kicking at a briar that has caught your boot,
you swear under your breath
and the breeze carries the curse to me.

My Father Watches
The Red Skelton Show

In my childhood home
in the darkened front room
my father and I watch *The Nutcracker* on TV
Apparitions of cinnamon from cream apple pies
my mother is baking
wander in from the kitchen,
and my father gives me a look to say
We'll sneak in there later for a sample.
The Christmas tree's blue, red, and green lights,
their paint chipped clear at the tips
from years of use,
draw me to the corner of the room
where I sit on the cold hardwood floor,
the nearby Seigler oil heater
straining to warm me.
Soon my father settles deeper into his chair
as his favorite show comes on,
and I hear the goofy voices of
Gertrude and Heathcliff,
and the audience laughs.
My father chuckles too
at the glowing screen.
And later Freddy the Freeloader,
my favorite hobo
who won't speak a word,
is into some mischief,
but I don't watch.
Instead I sit beneath the tree

and savor the smell of singed pine needles
that stick to the heated lights
while I stroke the silver tinsel—
fairies' hair—
that hangs on the limbs;
and I gaze at sparkling glass
balls and bells and clusters of grapes
that my mother and I have so carefully placed;
and I lift and squeeze the packages
of beautiful mystery
my mother has wrapped
and tied in curling crimped ribbon.
From this reverie
I am awakened
by the giggles of Red Skelton
and the laughter of my father—
both sounds as sweet
as Christmas.

Gathering Dirt

That spring
my mother and I gathered dirt
from the woods above my house;
she stuffed her burlap bags with the earth's
dead skin of pine needles, crumbled cones, and bark—
mulch as black as any gardener could desire;
and she hoed at the base of trees,
raking the dry stuff with
work-cracked fingers
(she said she'd never had pretty hands,
never been paid a compliment on them,
but I said they could be pretty if she wanted
and she laughed at the idea).
She preferred to use her hands:
chopping and stacking wood even in spring
to prepare for winter,
pulling weeds from her tulip bed,
planting onions, potatoes, and cabbage,
and all the crops a farmer could brag about
though hers were confined to a Victory garden
(the best kind, she swore, though the War was
long past).
And so in my bit of woods
she scraped the dirt and delighted in it
as some might in discovering gold dust,
for her treasure was the promise of
growing things
that would relish this soil and take pleasure
in her nurturing.
I helped her—

pressing down handfuls of black that she dropped in—
till I caught my thumb on a thorn and cried out.
"Here, let me do it," she said,
with no regard for her hands;
she would protect mine,
best suited for Chopin,
only gentle uses,
too soft to be practical,
too delicate to fondle the earth.

Her Sister's Shoes

As I cleaned my mother's closet
to help her discard the worn,
make room for the new,
I tossed aside her shoes,
outdated pumps and slick-bottomed sandals,
while she busied herself in dresser drawers.
I opened a box and discovered
a pair of oxfords,
most discardable of all,
I thought:
short, plain, gray—
I cast them aside
maybe with a laugh, some remark.
Suddenly,
she snatched them
and held them to her;
"They're Ruby's shoes!" she cried
and told me
they were all she had of her sister
who died many years ago.

I remembered:
my kind, portly, gruff-speaking aunt,
a cigarette dangling from her mouth,
ashes always dangerously hanging—
a sort of Shelley Winters
who loved me like a daughter
she never had.
Fourteen I was when she passed—
she barely fifty.
Yes, now those shoes I recalled:

work shoes for the textile mill;
ugly, functional,
yet they defined the simple nature
of the homely woman,
once a hazel-eyed beauty
much pursued in her time.
"God, why do some people die so young?
Why do their hearts give way?"
we'd asked then,
no comfort offered by preacher or kin.
All this I recalled—
passing by her casket in the Victorian parlor
of our town funeral home;
standing in line amidst the suffocating perfume
of rose-encircled wreaths,
hearing my mother in front of me
wailing—
as she had wailed from her bedroom
the nights before.
From down the hall
I heard my father trying to comfort her—
"Don't cry, don't cry—"
in a tender voice
reserved mostly for his children.
I pressed my palms hard over my ears,
put my head under the covers
to shut out the horror.

All this—all this—
brought back by two mute shoes
best left alone
in my mother's closet.

Player Piano

The player piano has lost its smell.
All my polishing of wood and scrubbing of ivory
have dissolved the mustiness
of decades in my grandmother's parlor.

Sometimes I dream of that front room,
the cool air and scent of mildew;
the white lace curtains
that let in shadows from the woods;
rose-patterned linoleum rug
and floral-print mohair couch
with hand-embroidered antimacassars—
a scene from the twenties,
suspended in time.

Here the piano sat,
its rubber tubing stripped for World War II,
its mechanism long destroyed;
the expression levers useless
to a child's curious fingers.
But the yellow, chipped keys
still offered a chiming sound
those Sunday evenings in the sixties
when I plunked hymns for my grandmother.

Today, in my house,
I press my nose to the closed mahogany lid
and stroke my hand across the sliding doors
that opened once to perforated rolls—
fox trots and waltzes—
and I inhale.
Gone, though, is the smell,
except in my mind,
in my memory of that room.

Garden Creek

The water held no more than rocks
and an occasional rusted hubcap that
washed from the filling station on the
other side of the creek bank.
The water was shallow and usually clear,
but dingy at times with silt.
Its fragrance was not of galax or pine
or other pungent or sweet smells
of mountain brooks;
all one smelled was the fumes of gasoline
from nearby pumps
or exhaust from cars on the highway.
Yet those days I sat content on the footbridge
that crossed my grandmother's creek
at the edge of her backyard—
a bridge made of two shaved logs and hand sawed boards,
with rotted holes big enough
for a dog's leg to get trapped in
or a child's foot;
a bridge made by my grandfather Matt,
long dead and known to me only
in pictures stored in a frayed Victorian album
or in an ornate framed portrait,
both hidden upstairs in a darkened room.
Those days I sat with a bamboo pole,
a line and maybe a safety pin for a hook,
the hook lightly carried downstream in the current.
I was patient, waiting for a fish that would never bite,
encouraged by sight of
an occasional salamander or frog.

A short walk away ran the muddy waters
of the Catawba River,
in its depths all the mud turtles, snakes,
catfish and carp
a seasoned fisherman might hate or hope to see,
one weary from the cotton mill
or carpentry job,
stealing some time,
leaning over the riverbank with Camel cigarette in mouth,
spinning rod in hand.
But on those warm summer days
in the 1960's
I preferred the quiet waters of Garden Creek,
my grandmother in the house
sitting in front of the black and white Zenith
watching *Video Village* hosted by Monty Hall—
her favorite show—
and I, alone, sitting on the bridge,
pole in hand, sneaking a look across the highway
towards the gently sloping street
where my parents, brother, dog, and I lived,
waiting for a fish to bite
and 3:30 to arrive
so my father would come
to take me home.

My Cousin

My cousin David hid under the bed
when the train rumbled by
years ago in that cotton mill house
where he lived with his mother and grandmother.
They tried to coax him out,
promised him nothing would harm him,
but he lay on his side,
knees cradled,
and they left him there
until the house stopped shaking
and the room was quiet again.
Rheumatic fever had retarded his mind
and damaged his heart,
destroyed his nerves so that in time
they couldn't keep him at home.
Pictures show him as a toddler,
flushed cheeks, shining brown eyes,
but even then
his gaze was guarded,
his eyes surprised.

At Christmas I go to see him
in the dingy rest home where he lives,
where he shares a room with three other men,
all of them begging quarters from me
before I can get out of my car;
my cousin taps my arm and motions me away,
babbling something I can't understand,

solicitous of my attention—
after all, my visit comes but once a year
and so few of his family are alive any more.

I mean to go more often,
and I think about him through the year,
but I tell myself he doesn't mind,
has his own life there and
too many visits would make him more nervous,
so I go at Christmas to discover him
smoking cigarettes he begs
and walking barefoot down the halls;
then I leave him in peace with his roommates,
with nurses who seem to care
for the most part.
But I think about him most often at night,
when I hear the train in the distance,
its whistle cutting the air,
its rumble in my body.
I pull the quilt to my chin,
closing my eyes and
holding my breath,
until the caboose has stolen into the mountains.

Eight O'Clock

When I was a girl
all we had to do was
walk in the front door
of my uncle Herbert's house
and I could smell the
pungent aroma of coffee brewing
and knew my uncle had
already laid out my cup, saucer,
and cake plate.
Oh, the lovely, delicious
cold-from-the-refrigerator
pastel-frosted cakes
he made
(for he loved to cook—
had done so in the Army;
grease-splattered T-shirt and pot belly
like Mel in the TV. show *Alice*,
though my uncle's diner was his own kitchen).

While my mother and aunt chatted elsewhere,
I sat in that kitchen
at my uncle's chipped Formica table
in his rented white frame house
on the wrong side of the Southern Railroad tracks,
and there I listened to the men talking—
my father and uncle—
heard of low wages in textile mills
and bad politicians
and football games
and I rested in the haze of Camel cigarette smoke,
relaxed, satisfied,
sipping my adult cup of Eight O'Clock coffee.

Porch Swing

They've taken down Cora's hanging baskets,
red geraniums, wandering Jew and fern,
and stacked her glider and chairs to the side,
only the white swing undisturbed.
And the green shades are pulled down
to keep curious eyes of neighborhood children
from spying the empty rooms within.

Living with her granddaughter—
too feeble now to live alone,
though she'd done so into her
ninety-first year,
twenty-some years a widow—
she's safe now.

But what does she think in the evenings,
whippoorwills calling in the hills
behind her house—
does she want to sit on her own porch
and watch the flickering lights of T.V.'s
reflected in the living rooms of neighboring houses—
as she so enjoyed doing—
or early in the day, before the Southern heat
drives us in,
when dew lies on the grass and a light breeze stirs,
does she want to sit in her swing
and peel a peach,
as she was wont to do
on summer mornings?

We asked her granddaughter's husband,
Couldn't she come back sometimes
just to sit on her porch,
for we missed seeing her there.
But he said it would hurt her to come,
best to stay at her new home and adjust.

I asked my mother if she'd like to visit her,
go over with some fruit,
news of the street,
but she said, "It won't be the same."
Yet as I drive to visit my parents,
I can't help but look to that bare porch,
the empty white swing
that I've swung in as a child,
and think of Cora sitting there
stringing green beans with my mother
while I play in the yard.

Slingshot

He may have scared other children from his yard,
thrown rocks at their dogs,
and threatened to call the pound.
He might have summoned the law on his neighbors
for allowing a tree limb to fall on his land
or chickens to wander into his garden—
this may all be true.
But for me he made a slingshot,
cut the fork of a laurel tree,
whittled notches with cigarette-stained fingers,
attached strips of rubber, an old shoe tongue,
and sat with me in his porch swing
to show me how to aim it.

To me he told tales of fishing
in the Catawba River,
and he fried catfish that he'd caught,
inviting me to sit at his table
with him and his wife Cora.

Yet I still hear stories of his meanness,
ill will toward neighbors,
so hard for them to understand
of a Baptist deacon.

But in my mind I see him
grin sidewise at me,
pretending to pull a nickel from my ear
or crack a flea—*click*—
between his thumbnail and fingernail
and then pinch my ear lobe,
gently,
for good measure.

Silo

The silo peers out at me,
nearly hidden in the dogwood-laced hillside,
and I almost drive off the highway
trying to see it better.
Has it always been there?
I've never noticed,
but it is so much like one I've known before
that it makes me turn my head.

Weeks I go,
my mind focused inward,
not noticing much around me.
But the silo sets me to thinking
and studying every pasture
of fescue and clover,
wishing I could call some field my own,
some hill bordered by dogwood trees,
like the land my grandmother's grandfather Alex
must have pictured
on the journey here from Ireland.

An Endless Tapestry

A child,
I pricked my hands on the barbed wire
that meant to keep me from the farmer's land
as I stretched the strands to get inside.
I trudged through briary grass, past dogwoods,
till I reached the clear slope above the silo,
where I gathered a handful of clover flowers
and strung them for a necklace.
I knew these beads belonged to someone else,
but I had to make them mine.

In that silo,
nagging me like a promise,
I am reminded of my need:
I want to call its dome my own,
stand in its evening shadow
and call the shadow mine.
It's the land that tugs at me again,
the grass, the trees, the clover.

My Daughter Ponders Death

"Mommy not going away?"
she asks—
her three-year-old voice
just now hinting the inflections
of a Southern accent,
her native tongue
lost in the recesses of her memory—
and she pulls at my dress tail
as I make preparations to leave for work.
"Mommy coming back?"
"Yes, Dear, I will," I say
as I've said every evening I've left her
in her father's care
these weeks since her grandmother's death.
"Mommy not die,"
one evening she asserted.
"No, honey, not soon I hope."
But there are no guarantees,
I think.
Oh, she's started through the
dark tunnel of worry
as I started when I wasn't much older.
I recall lying in the bed
of my first babysitter—
a kind elderly neighbor woman
whose front room in winter
was heated by a coal stove.
My father drove me there before daylight,
carried me into her house,
and left me safe in her tall, soft bed.

I lay covered by quilts with my feet soles
pressed on the towel-wrapped brick
she had heated for me;
and in the drowse
of the cold, dark room
I began to think:
What if my father didn't come back?
What if he and my mother died today?
(For it always seemed they would go together
as surely as they worked together in the hosiery mill.)
Then I would squeeze the tears in my eyes
until I fell asleep.
And so it went
all those earliest mornings of my childhood;
and later in the classroom,
on the playground,
in my own bed at night,
my brother lightly snoring beside me,
I worried.

Now my daughter
has picked up my old habit of troubling
over the uncontrollable.
Is it her fear of abandonment,
stirred by some recollection of being left alone
in that faraway land
of Carpathian Mountains and aging castles?
Or her blood knowledge of fast moves
and sudden departures
from campfires in Romany caravans?
Or is it this last
and more dear departure of

her new and trusted kin?
For surely she's seen the palpable grief
in our house
since my husband's mother's death;
heard the questions spoken to the air—
"Why now?"
"Couldn't she have lived longer?"—
and witnessed the lowering of heads,
heard the prolonged silences broken
by an occasional recollection
and moment of laughter
or resignation into sighs
or quiet weeping.
She's absorbed it all.
And so now she asks
"Mommy not leaving?"
"Not for long," I say, pulling my hand
from her brown hand's grasp,
hoping I'm true to my word
and in time her mind will rest.

Ritual

In bed,
my daughter snuggles her bottom
back against my belly,
and says, "Tell me a story."
So I reach to brush her dark curls
from her face,
and when she settles in,
her heels wedged
between my legs for warmth,
her thumb in mouth,
I begin.
The easy ones first:
Red Riding Hood
(modified to feature her in
leading role),
Three Bears;
then the family tales:
the time my mother
when a girl
carried a chicken from her
cousin's house in the country
miles into town
only to lose it along the way
to a flock of local chickens;
my father sixty years ago
watching dolphins play
alongside a merchant ship
in some foreign sea.
But as I start to ease away,
when her breathing seems steady,

she suddenly says,
"Again."
And for lack of another tale,
I say,
"I'll tell you what your pa told me
when I was about your age—
three years old—
when I would crawl in bed
with him on Sunday nights
after *Bonanza*..."
and leaning close to her cheek,
I say slowly, deliberately,
"...Friends, Romans, countrymen
lend me your ears!"
and I can't help but laugh
recalling how he recited it
those faraway Sundays—
his intention to tickle me
with the silly possibility of those words—
and Annie giggles,
picking up the foolishness.
And she says "Again,"
so I tell it,
milking it for what it's worth,
until I hear her light snoring
and see that her dark-lashed eyes
have closed for the night.
I lift her into her crib,
cover her, and wonder:
Will she learn to love Shakespeare
as I have,
being teased with his lines

but reminded in time—
as my father was certain to remind me—
of more earnest
meanings in Mark Antony's speech?
Will she remember this ritual?
No matter;
she is finally asleep
and I can get on with my evening's chores.
But later as I turn to fold clothes,
warm from the dryer,
I hear my father's voice—
its mock-profound tone—
Friends, Romans, countrymen...
and again he makes me laugh.

II

An Endless Tapestry

My world is a painted fresco, where coloured shapes
Of old, ineffectual lives linger blurred and warm;
An endless tapestry the past has woven drapes
The halls of my life, compelling my soul to conform.

Dreams Nascent, D. H. Lawrence

Fate

She believed in the old ways—
didn't put stock in modern notions
of coincidence or in confused explanations
of the *odd* that a teacher might offer.
It was powers she'd heard of as a child,
such as the placing of a hand on a wart
and rubbing in some concoction
passed down from mama to daughter
to remove the growth,
that she trusted.
It was a gift some women had—
her own great aunt witness to
such magic
though she died from the taking of her mole—
melanoma a doctor would say;
Why did she let someone tamper with
it that way?
Yet still that death didn't change
her family's belief in the power.
So when she first saw the man on Main Street
and knew beyond a shadow of a doubt
that he was what she wanted,
she searched her mind for recollections
of tales told in her earliest days—
whispered stories on summer front porches
of fireballs and panthers
and spells—
and she set her mind on getting him.
In the shadows of her cold room at night
for two solid weeks

she lit a candle
and held her hand up
as if taking a vow
or swearing an oath
and closed her blue eyes tight.
Think about me, she whispered
and held the image of his face
in her mind.
Want me, she said,
(*as I want you*).
She chanted this until the wee hours,
her throat so sore she couldn't swallow
and until the candle wick drowned in the
pool of wax and she was left
in moonless dark.
In bed, warmed by a covering of quilts
her great-grandma had stitched
eighty years before,
she thought of the man's dark eyes,
his curly black hair;
his clean, crisply laundered white shirt
and overcoat
that a banker wore.
And she forgot that he might feel
too good for the likes of her
(why, down their noses
the tellers looked
when she sneaked in to get a glimpse
of him).
Never mind.
A December Friday evening when she
stood outside the First National Bank

and waited for him to come out
of the tall glass doors,
low and behold
he stepped outside
stood on the street
and looked straight at her
though she didn't call his name
Fate (such a fine and pretty name!)
and he held her gaze.
His eyes did not leave hers for some time.
Thank you, Lord,
she said,
looking up into the gray sky,
her eyes blurred with tears;
Thank you, Lord
(though she knew Jesus might not have been
the cause of her good fortune)
and she held her hand over her heart
for a moment
and then over her mouth
to cover the grin that she couldn't stop.
He took an interest in me,
she thought
and watched him turn and walk down the street,
cut the corner by the Rexall Drug Store
and disappear.
I'll have you in my bed before it's over,
my darlin' Fate,
she thought
and started the long walk home.

Far Pasture

I sit on the old woman's back porch,
where we talk of canning and the lonesome feeling
you get after Christmas,
especially when the pastures are brown
but the sun is warm,
as it is today;
then we look out over her garden,
a tangled patch of dried cornstalks and vines,
and beyond her fields to the bleached, bare poplars
and scraggly pines;
she says she's partial to that far pasture
her husband tended so carefully,
more fondly than he handled his children,
but she wishes it weren't taken by broom sage
and milkweed,
though summer honeysuckle's not so bad—
she recalls sipping its nectar
when she was a girl.
"Will your daughter ever move back here?" I ask,
and she pats the arm of her rocking chair,
the green paint worn brittle by such patting,
and says, "Well, no, I don't expect so,"
telling me by her tone she's given it some thought.
"It's a pretty place," I say and look at her,
and she nods to put an end to the subject.

Mountain Boy

His oversized coat, black and moth-eaten,
reminds me of Lincoln's,
but I know it was handed down
from one of those brothers who,
unlike him,
stare out the torn screen door of their leaning shack
and watch me as I rock on my front porch
or hang my wet clothes over the railing.
I turn my face
to avoid their stares.
But he catches my gaze—
gaunt, pale-eyed mountain boy,
too old for school,
too simple for society,
with his stooping walk into the woods,
shotgun on his shoulder.
I wave at him,
hoping the gesture will disarm him,
yet knowing his family will distrust me more;
but something in his reluctance to look my way,
while his brothers gawk without shame,
makes me reach out to him
as I did to the fawn that stole into my garden
or the sparrow hawk
whose broken wing I mended.

Wedding Day

Beyond the window,
where light slipped in
and made the lace patterns
glow with late evening rose,
lay fields and farther still
a split rail fence and then
mountains where his property ended.
They sat on his feather bed
and heard voices in the kitchen—
laughter of women who scraped
cast iron skillets
and stoked the wood stove's belly,
their wedding supper
being stirred and baked;
and talk of men, more hushed,
their tobacco smoke curling through the house.
To this room they had stolen
and sat where tonight they would lie,
his glance both bold and shy
telling her what the setting sun would bring,
when the noises in the kitchen
and the light faded away.

Lists

Winter morning, frost on the grass and roof;
the old pickup truck chugs in the shed beside the house,
and he grips the wheel, adjusts his glasses,
and stares at a gas gauge that doesn't work.
Don't need nothing from the store, he thinks;
No point in wasting gas.
He just wants to make sure it'll still start.

He walks into the kitchen where his wife kneads dough;
"You can't beat a GMC," he says and
she thinks, punching the mound,
Sourwood honey. Black strap molasses. Fresh sweetmilk.
These, too, you couldn't beat.
She thought in lists now, as earlier that morning
while she hung out clothes
that stiffened when the air hit them:
Bed sheet—tore in the center. Pillowcase.
Jack's handkerchief—can't wash out blood.
And she looked around her:
Snow clouds. Apple tree—icy limbs bow to the sky.
Jack's hound dog—no, woodpile.

Stretching the dough, patting it thin,
and folding it like a baby's diaper,
she hears him cough from his forty-year-old cold,
"You can't beat...," he says again.
No, that's the truth, she thinks,
and nods her head.

Visit from Her Son

She leans over her oil heater
to catch the rising waves of heat
and gazes at the mantelpiece,
dust from two years back
clouding the framed pictures
and layering the embroidered scarves;
she's meant to attend to that,
but her fall's put an end to such work.
And she notices that the clock has stopped,
yet she knows that her son will come
to sit with her and talk,
arms crossed like the law;
and she'll lend him a few dollars again,
ignoring his complaints
that the room is stifling
and she needs to walk with her cane
and it's not right her living alone.
She'll ignore him as always—
all a person can do
when them that have no business to talk
keep on talking just the same.

Seed Catalog

No letter today—
she has looked in the mailbox,
the lid so frosty it sticks to her fingers—
not a note, no post card,
no hint that anyone cares she's alive;
just a seed catalog,
one hundred and thirty pages in vivid color:
Better Boy tomatoes,
Calla Queen begonias,
the common and the rare,
displayed for her convenience.
She will place her order early
(bonus seeds if she does)
and wait for her package
(guaranteed to come by planting time).
But when she stands at the mailbox
each morning until springtime,
it won't be seeds she longs to find.

Brown Lung

He called her in the night,
between the coughing and spitting,
for a glass of water,
a little company in the darkness.
She pulled open his curtains
to let in the moonlight,
told him to think on the stars
and he would rest.
But what he wanted was her touch,
to lay his head against her breast,
but he settled for her palm on his brow
though she found his skin damp
and drew her hand away.
"Think on the stars," she said.
"Picture the Big Dipper."
Then she closed the door behind her.
He wanted to talk about the cotton dust
that fell in the mill like dirty snow;
but he wouldn't call her back—
never troubled her twice in one night—
so she went to her bed and slept.

March Flowers

We call them March flowers
though a book would say *daffodils*—
splash of yellow on a late-winter landscape,
sometimes in sunlight or tipped by snow,
gone almost as soon as they came.
You can see patches in a pasture
and know that's where a homeplace stood
where a woman carried water from a well,
a man split kindling for a fire.
Like tombstones, the yellow bells
tell stories about the past.
To the wind they breathe their sweetness,
whisper their secrets.

Patchwork

They were given patchwork quilts at their wedding,
the custom in those parts;
quilts of varying designs to fit the seasons:
russet corn shock, amber pumpkin for autumn;
balsam fir and mistletoe for winter;
hand-stitched for their marriage bed.

Boy and girl of the mountains,
yesterday they watched the hawk seize its sparrow
while they roamed the fields, a wildness in their eyes.
Today they study the pasture that must be plowed.

Tilling and hoeing, they labor together,
though she longs for the travail of a child,
imagines its face while she scatters seeds in furrows,
while she rests a moment in the sun.

Tonight he lies with her in the dark,
where they sleep beneath a patchwork quilt
of flowering dogwood and pink azalea;
he dreams of the crops they will gather,
she of the life that he has sown.

Sparrow Hawk

The sparrow hawk became his friend,
though distrusting him at first,
not seeing that when the man found it
entangled in fishing line in the field
near the river,
he meant it anything but harm.
But it softened
as he sat in the dark room beside it.
Silent, his eyes turned away,
he let it discover that he held it captive
only because he cared
and would offer freedom when
May hills were green and the air warm.
Trust came when he fed it chicken
and trained it to fly from his fist
at field mice and grasshoppers,
building its strength and confidence
to face the sky again.
He was loath, though, to give it back
to the distant Blue Ridge,
saddened to think he wouldn't hear its chirp
or feel the light talons as it lit on his head
or see the solemn brown gaze.
Yet when it flew from his hand,
vanished beyond the stirring pines,
he, too, lifted his arms to catch the breeze.

Earth

All around her was the smell of earth,
rich as freshly plowed ground,
pungent as the marigolds that grew at her water pump.
We sat on her screened-in porch and snapped green beans,
she sneaking a raw one into her mouth.
She never questioned eating them off the vine,
dirt-smeared bitter things,
and I imitated her, though Mother would fuss
if she knew—
bad for digestion, caused worms or something.
But she never cared, and ate raw peas,
bit with strong teeth into juicy hard potatoes
as soon as she'd crunch an apple.
For she liked the taste of the earth,
said she always had, just like her papa
who'd sample the furrow before planting;
she recalled him with mud on his chin
as brown as tobacco spit.
Something familiar about the taste of earth,
she said,
almost like it was part of us.

I remembered this later
when I tossed a clod down onto her,
the others tossing a carnation from the wreaths.
No, she'd want the earth—
close to her like a quilt,
restful as an embrace.

Apples

Shaking the apples from the tree,
an apron around her waist,
she brings me face to face with death.
An old woman embracing the bark,
she pushes and the speckled fruit falls,
splattering, too mellow, about her feet.
Such apples come and then they're gone
one day, it seems,
with the seasons.

Tennessee Baptism, 1915

The preacher, in striped shirt and suspenders,
stands in the muddy river,
water soaking his thighs;
his left hand grips the woman's clasped hands,
his right hand is uplifted;
eyes closed, he prays to the blackening sky.
His congregation waits on the bank:
women, in long skirts and boots,
hold black umbrellas;
men, arms crossed, heads bent
beneath broad-brimmed hats,
Sunday best,
wait for the storm to pass;
and children watch, too:
boys in overalls and floppy hats sit barefoot
on the riverbank
while girls in white dresses and oversized hats
peer around their mothers;
all gathered to see
the dark-haired woman,
whose head is bowed,
eyes closed,
who waits for the preacher's hand
to cover her mouth and nose—
the quick wet immersion,
the washing of her soul.

Tent Revival

The boy waded barefoot through the wet pasture
to reach the lantern light of the tent revival.
Sneaking in, he sat on a bench in shadows,
inhaled the mix of sweat, tobacco, whiskey,
and lavender water,
and listened to the preacher's words:
"I ask you, Brethren, what is Hell?"
The boy pondered this question,
recalled talk of fire and burning,
but now he felt chilled
by the night drizzle
and noticed where a briar had caught his ankle,
the beads of red just starting to sting,
and he thought to himself:
Hell must be cold;
being barefoot when you need shoes,
briars and copperheads lurking in the grass.
And he wished he were home again,
across the pitch-dark pasture,
quiet beneath his blanket,
thinking of nothing but sleep.

Prayer for Rain

The people gathered on the hill
above the Baptist church
to pray for rain.

Men, in dusty overalls and wide-brimmed hats,
women, in aprons crusted with dough,
and children, barefoot and fretful from the heat,
stood in the sun and waited.

The preacher, whose idea it was to gather,
held the Bible high,
and with mind lost in Scripture,
he said:
"Elias prayed 'and the heaven gave rain,
and the earth brought forth her fruit';
Lord, we ask the same,
for our ground has cracked
and our hearts grow weary."

And so they stood.

When the drops splattered on plows
unattended by the sheds
and hissed on tin roofs and plopped in dust,
the mules shifted in their stalls,
ears back and eyes white;
and the church bell rang,
echoing through the valley,
heard even by cows in distant dry pastures,
who lifted their heads to listen.